ROCK HITS

INSTRUMENTAL PLAY-ALONG

Violin

INSTRUMENTAL PLAY-ALONG

ROCK HITS

Violin

SOLO ARRANGEMENTS OF 15 CLASSIC SONGS WITH CD ACCOMPANIMENT

HOW TO USE THE CD ACCOMPANIMENT:
A melody cue appears on the right channel only.
If your CD player has a balance adjustment, you can adjust the volume of the melody by turning down the right channel.

This publication is not authorised for sale in the United States of America and/or Canada

HAL LEONARD EUROPE
DISTRIBUTED BY MUSIC SALES

Exclusive Distributors:
Music Sales Limited
14-15 Berners Street, London W1T 3LJ, UK.

Order No. HLE90002880
ISBN-13: 978-1-84609-372-2
ISBN-10: 1-84609-372-4
This book © Copyright 2007 Hal Leonard Europe

Unauthorised reproduction of any part of this publication by any means including photocopying is an infringement of copyright.

Printed in the USA

Your Guarantee of Quality
As publishers, we strive to produce every book to the highest commercial standards. The book has been carefully designed to minimise awkward page turns and to make playing from it a real pleasure. Throughout, the printing and binding have been planned to ensure a sturdy, attractive publication which should give years of enjoyment. If your copy fails to meet our high standards, please inform us and we will gladly replace it.

www.musicsales.com

Contents

TITLE	ARTIST	PAGE	CD TRACK
Aqualung	Jethro Tull	6	1
Best Of My Love	The Eagles	8	2
The Boys Are Back In Town	Thin Lizzy	10	3
Brown Eyed Girl	Van Morrison	11	4
Crocodile Rock	Elton John	12	5
Don't Stop	Fleetwood Mac	14	6
Fly Like An Eagle	Steve Miller Band	16	7
Free Bird	Lynyrd Skynyrd	15	8
Gimme Some Lovin'	The Spencer Davis Group	18	9
I Want You To Want Me	Cheap Trick	20	10
Low Rider	War	22	11
Maggie May	Rod Stewart	23	12
Owner Of A Lonely Heart	Yes	28	13
Walk This Way	Aerosmith	24	14
White Wedding	Billy Idol	26	15
B♭ Tuning Notes			16

AQUALUNG

VIOLIN

Music by IAN ANDERSON
Lyrics by JENNIE ANDERSON

Copyright © 1971 Chrysalis Music Ltd.
Copyright Renewed
All Rights for the U.S. and Canada Administered by Chrysalis Music
All Rights Reserved   Used by Permission

BEST OF MY LOVE

Words and Music by JOHN DAVID SOUTHER, DON HENLEY and GLENN FREY

BROWN EYED GIRL

Words and Music by
VAN MORRISON

5 CROCODILE ROCK

VIOLIN

Words and Music by ELTON JOHN and BERNIE TAUPIN

Light-hearted Rock

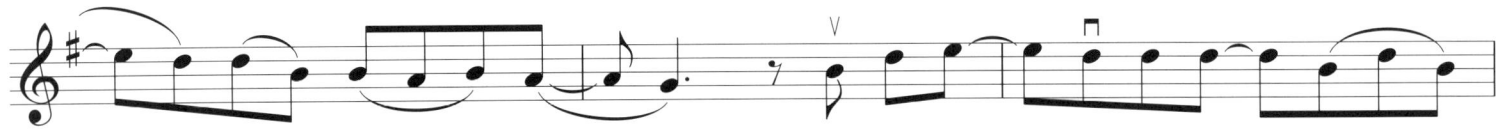

Copyright © 1972 UNIVERSAL /DICK JAMES MUSIC LTD.
Copyright Renewed
All Rights for the United States and Canada Controlled and Administered by UNIVERSAL - SONGS OF POLYGRAM INTERNATIONAL, INC.
All Rights Reserved   Used by Permission

Don't Stop

VIOLIN

Words and Music by
CHRISTINE McVIE

Moderate Rock Shuffle

FLY LIKE AN EAGLE

VIOLIN

Words and Music by STEVE MILLER

Copyright © 1976 by Sailor Music
Copyright Renewed
All Rights Reserved   Used by Permission

GIMME SOME LOVIN'

Words and Music by SPENCER DAVIS,
MUFF WINWOOD and STEVE WINWOOD

VIOLIN

Copyright © 1967 Island Music Ltd. and F.S. Music Ltd.
Copyright Renewed
All Rights for Island Music Ltd. in the U.S. and Canada Administered by Songs Of PolyGram International, Inc.
All Rights for F.S. Music Ltd. in the U.S. and Canada Administered by Warner-Tamerlane Publishing Corp.
International Copyright Secured   All Rights Reserved

LOW RIDER

Violin

Words and Music by SYLVESTER ALLEN, HAROLD R. BROWN, MORRIS DICKERSON, JERRY GOLDSMITH, LEROY JORDAN, LEE OSKAR, CHARLES W. MILLER and HOWARD SCOTT

Copyright © 1975 FAR OUT MUSIC, INC.
Copyright Renewed
All Rights Controlled and Administered by UNIVERSAL - POLYGRAM INTERNATIONAL PUBLISHING, INC.
All Rights Reserved   Used by Permission

MAGGIE MAY

Violin

Words and Music by ROD STEWART and MARTIN QUITTENTON

WALK THIS WAY

Words and Music by STEVEN TYLER
and JOE PERRY

Copyright © 1977 Music Of Stage Three
All Rights Reserved   Used by Permission

WHITE WEDDING

VIOLIN

Words and Music by
BILLY IDOL

Fast Rock

Copyright © 1982 Chrysalis Music and Boneidol Music
All Rights Administered by Chrysalis Music
All Rights Reserved   Used by Permission